Tom Roz:

Digital Transformation

Tom Rozsas

Digital Transformation

Phoenix Books
Budapest, 2021

Develop mindfulness to thrive in a transforming world

Getting Started with Meditation is a fast track introduction to a simple meditation practice that works. Meditation helps millions to reduce stress, face challenges, and live a happier life. Besides, it does not require special skills or abilities, costs only a few minutes of your time a day, and works for everyone. Follow the right practice, and meditation will improve your health, well-being, and help you tackle difficulties in all fields of life.

Meditation is simple, but it takes time to develop a solid practice and see the first results. Follow the wrong practice, and you will be distracted. This book helps you start with a simple, effective practice that you can start now, and customize to your needs when as you gain experience later.

Tom Rozsas
Getting Started with Mediation
is available on Amazon in all markets
or
you can download the e-book version free from
www.tomrozsas.com

Contents

Foreword

Digital transformation is the secret weapon of managers today. They expect it to breathe new life in the organization and boost performance. With the ubiquity of digital technology and prevalence of the internet, it comes naturally that digitalization is both a necessity and solution to many problems. This is true. But to succeed, we need to understand the challenge.

Managers often consider digital transformation a simple technical modernization exercise. Yet, organizations often struggle to realize expected benefits from implementing systems from the Gartner Magic Quadrant.[1] Transformation projects stuck. Systems making others successful prove useless in their case. Projects derail, burn resources, and generate more problems than they solve.

Why organizations often struggle with these simple technical projects? Because they chose the wrong approach. Their perspective is wrong. They want a quick solution, a simple investment in technology. Managers often look at digital transformation as replacing some obsolete machine with a new one. They render transformation a simple system implementation project.

In this book, I show why this approach is wrong. I start with explaining what digital transformation is and why it is not a simple technical project. I show how deep is its effect on organizations and what role IT should play.

Then we size up the digital transformation endeavor exploring its entire reach. We look below the water-line to see the total mass of the iceberg. We understand the role of technology in the transformation and we see how far beyond we must look to succeed. Last, we look at how should we define digital transformation programs and projects how should we manage them.

This short book is only a primer to digital transformation. I cannot discuss topics in detail. But it helps to avoid the trap causing most trouble in digitalization: taking transformation as a technical project.

I also show that digital transformation is a lot more exciting. Systems consist not only of hardware and software. People, human interactions, and processes are far more important. If we explore these dimensions, we have a better chance to succeed. Enjoy the exploration and see what are the genuine sources of the benefits of digital transformation.

THE BASICS

TOM ROZSAS

New tricks of an old dog

Digital transformation became so pervasive in business vocabulary we forget it took momentum only in the past decade.[2] No wonder CEOs and managers face many misconceptions in its application and efforts to transform organizations often cannot deliver expected results.

What is digital transformation? Why the term emerged so late while we had the first electronic computers in the 1950s and personal computers in the 1970s? A brief history of computing will help us get the answer.

Digital transformation is a magic spell of business management today. Companies expect miracles from digitalization, considering it a universal tool to improve competitiveness. Software houses come out with solutions to an increasing range of business problems. Managers see these solutions as ready-made patches solving problems by a simple implementation.

Results often fall short of expectations. Ready-made solutions take a lot more time and effort to implement and efficiency gains are also lagging expected improvement. Yet digital transformation grips its appeal. Confidence in the concept despite its mediocre performance may stem from its novelty. Despite its ubiquitous presence, we are still learning digital transformation. Why is the concept a novelty half a century after the start of the digital revolution? Let us look at the history of computing to understand this puzzle.

Digital technology relies on the use of miniature electronic switches called transistors. The first transistor appeared in 1947, and transistors replaced electromechanical components in computers in the 1950s. The first monolithic integrated circuit or microchip, the ancestor of today's CPUs, appeared in 1959 leading to the first single chip microprocessor by Intel in 1971.

As technology developed, microchips had an increasing number of transistors. Chips in the 1960s had up to five hundred transistors. This number grew to twenty thousands in the 1970s, passed one million by mid 1980s and it is way over ten billions in the advanced processors today.

The 1970s was a turbulent decade with several computers designed for personal, educational or home use leading to the first IMB PC in 1981. Altair 8800 (in 1975), Apple II (1977), Atari 400/800 (1981), and Sinclair ZX80 are among the most notable home computers of the time. They were used for simple games and to learn to program.

The rivalry of Apple II and IBM PC successors started a revolution. While Apple had its own operating system, IBM used PC DOS from Microsoft, which they also licensed to other computer manufacturers as MS DOS.

Microsoft Windows appeared as Microsoft's answer to the first successful graphical user interface sold with Apple Macintosh computers from 1984. However, IBM PC clones with Microsoft operating systems dominated the market. Version 3.0, the first popular version of Microsoft Windows, appeared in 1990.

Portable versions evolved parallel to desktop computers. Maybe the first laptop following a modern form factor was the Toshiba T1100 in 1985. Personal computers continued to develop and become ubiquitous in households over the years.

From the mid-2000s, smartphones also appeared on the scene and became a success. Today, smartphones has computing power beyond that of large server computers of earlier days combined with great graphical displays and connectivity on-the-go.

Networks for communication are also essential for digital transformation. Development of computer networks started in the late 1960s already and gained momentum with the ascent of home computers.

The first internet service providers appeared in the late 1980s, the first web server and web browser in 1990. In the next fifteen years, internet use spread around the world. The term Web 2.0, websites based on user generated content, first appeared in 1999. San Francisco gave place to the first Web 2.0 Conference in 2004. Twitter and Facebook appeared in 2006. Web 2.0 is important for digital transformation, as it considers web technology as a platform for cooperation and not only a way to let information be available.

Prices dropped parallel to technological development. Computing power and communication bandwidth became cheap commodities instead of scarce resources. Information technology became pervasive.

With computers on every desktop, the need for support services and service management appeared. IT needed processes more than capital or new technology. For automation of business processes the need for exploring, modeling, and defining business activities also appeared. Instead of computers and communication bandwidth, IT professionals with business acumen became the scarce resource.

Standardization and modeling of IT services paved the way for modeling other business activities as well. With the pervasiveness of computing and communication technology and the spread of the business analysis discipline, all elements stood together with the perfect storm in business transformation.

Technology was the driving force behind the digital revolution in the first few decades. With Web 2.0, however, digital revolution arrived at a turning point. Web technology as a platform was ready and mature enough for something new. When user generated content becomes the focus for customers and businesses alike, technology alone can no longer lead the transformation. Business must catch up and take the lead.

IT alone can clear a path to general administration and computer use. Transforming enterprise processes, however, require business expertise in finance, accounting, manufacturing, product development, marketing, or project management. Business professionals must understand and model their own activities and take the lead in further evolution.

Digital transformation is a phrase describing the latest phase of the digital revolution. It covers the transformation of business processes around new models enabled by advanced digital technology.

As we have seen, digital transformation needs a lot more than computing power. No wonder it is a capstone of a long process spreading over several decades.

Technology is only one layer of the transformation process. We explore others in the rest of the book. First, we inspect the concept itself.

What is digital transformation?

Let us look closer at the concept of digital transformation. In this chapter, we start with the simple view many managers still look at digital transformation. Then I show a more precise perspective, which also shows why a simplistic view leads to problems.

In the second half of the chapter, I point to the radical change making digital transformation disruptive. I end the chapter with projecting the implications.

Digital transformation often interpreted as a system implementation project. Management often looks at benchmark organizations when trying to solve efficiency problems. When they find an information system at the core of re-engineered business processes, they assume the essential component is the IT solution itself. Their own organization can replicate success by implementing the same system.

With the illusion of possessing a quick solution, they push for a system implementation project. They often blame IT for not implementing such a solution earlier. If they get the green light, the first implementation project soon cascades into multiple system implementation and interface development projects with limited overall efficiency gains and much headache.

Why is it so? The problem has two layers. The first layer is about our tools. Information systems are only complicated tools. They do not solve problems; they help us solve them. Implementing an advanced information system is comparable to piloting a huge robot with powerful arms, fingers and legs multiplying our own capabilities.

Sure we can complete a lot more work in the cockpit of this machine provided we can control it. But to control robotic arms ten times the reach and power of our own, our moves must be ten times more precise and skillful. Otherwise we end up becoming an elephant in the China shop.

The second layer is about selecting the right tool to our task at hand. Successful organizations look at their processes first. They break down the organization's mission to integrated processes. They define the boundaries and connections of processes, model activities, and select tools to support them. The driving force is re-engineering processes around redefined business models and not the implementation of some new information system.

Digital transformation is a fundamental change in how we make business and not a simple application of new technology to old ways of working. Technology enables the change. But remodeling our business is the core of digital transformation.

Figure 1 below captures the essence of this paradigm shift. Advanced digital technology enables a fresh way of cooperation. Instead of possessing information only about their task at hand and sharing information through cascading transactions, contributors rely on the same shared model and information available to all. Not only there is a single source of truth for everyone, but the propagation time of information is zero within the organization.

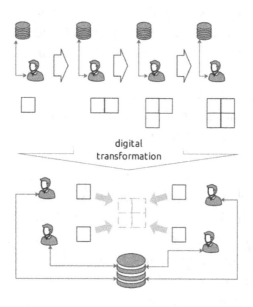

Figure 1. The essence of the paradigms shift behind digital transformation.

This change has far-reaching implications. Immediate access to relevant information enables efficient processes but also requires novel approaches and models. Cooperation of contributors also needs new foundations.

Besides, organizations cannot limit digital transformation to selected processes only. While digital transformation may be gradual proceeding from system to system, re-engineering must transfuse the entire organization.

Efficiency gains do not derive from system implementations, but new processes and a fresh approach to cooperation enabled by advanced technology. The paradigms shift also affects culture. In a world where information, including mistakes, propagates with infinite speed and accessed by all stakeholders, trust and cooperation are key. Contributors can correct mistakes fast, but managers cannot hold power positions based on the monopoly of information. Managers need to empower contributors and focus on process improvements and removing obstacles instead of withholding information for decision making.

Digital transformation is not about system implementation. It is not even about a roadmap for consecutive system implementations. Digital transformation is about the complete renewal of businesses under a new paradigm advanced technology brought about. It starts with embracing the new paradigm. It requires fundamental cultural change and ends in a complete overhaul of business models and processes.

Effects on the organization

Digital transformation has a deep impact on organizations. It may start as a strategic initiative or an accidental system implementation project for partial efficiency gain. It only ends when the entire organization gets transformed. A partial effort not only cannot realize benefits hoped for but also leaves the organization off-balance, and in transition.

Digital transformation is cross-functional. We cannot limit transformation to a single functional unit or area in the organization. Think about value chains. Figure 2 displays a general value chain model. Functional processes are interconnected in the value chain. If we re-engineer the processes of a single functional area without adjusting others, we compromise efficiency gains.

We only shift bottlenecks elsewhere by speeding processes in a single area, even if boundaries and interfaces between functional areas and support systems are clear.

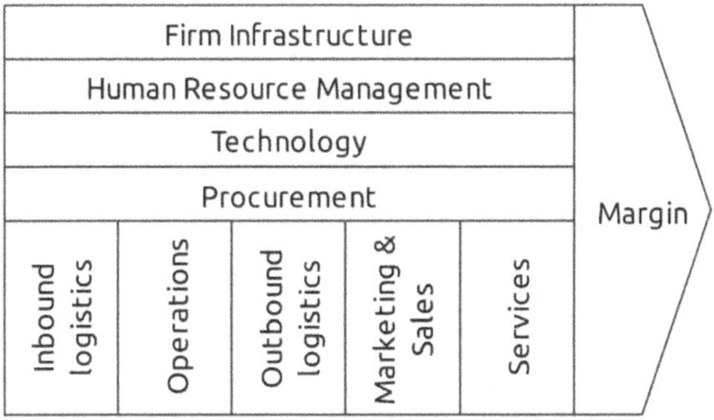

Firm Infrastructure					Margin
Human Resource Management					
Technology					
Procurement					
Inbound logistics	Operations	Outbound logistics	Marketing & Sales	Services	

Figure 2. Porter's value chain[3]

Because of cross-functionality, silos are incompatible with digital transformation. Automation of processes in one field involves interfaces to adjacent systems. Technology enables smooth information flow and information integrity, presuming we do not set barriers between functional areas.

With integrated systems, we can preserve information integrity by capturing all data at the place of their origin, and make them available to all. When silos hide their piece of the puzzle, they force others to fall back on decisions based on assumptions.

Digital transformation shall be complete to work. If not the entire organization, the strategic business unit must be transformed to avoid bottlenecks compromising overall benefits. While some units may pioneer the process, the vision of transformation must be complete.

The goal of digital transformation is to realize the potential of the paradigm shift brought about by the advance of technology. An active cooperation and shared information replacing rigid functional boundaries is at the core of this change.

Isolated, non-participating units halt the transformation unless they are redundant and should be dissolved. Mixing transformed and traditional units in the same organization leads to conflicts and tension. The choice is going forward, transforming the entire organization, or halting the process and fail.

The depth of change is also characteristic to digital transformation. Systems can help organizations to achieve desired results if stakeholders and contributors accept the new paradigm. Digital transformation provides means to share information and make decisions based on the same set of information at all levels.

But to share information, functions must be ready to give up their power from the monopoly of information. This requires an approach the Arbinger Institute[4] calls outward mindset. As shown on Figure 3, people with and outward mindset focus on common results instead of their partial interests.

An outward mindset is essential for successful digital transformation. Technology only enables collaboration based on mutual contribution. It does not enforce it.

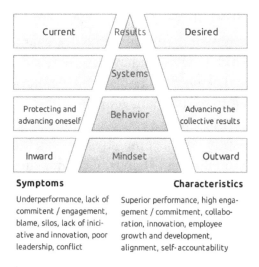

Symptoms	Characteristics
Underperformance, lack of commitent / engagement, blame, silos, lack of iniciative and innovation, poor leadership, conflict	Superior performance, high engagement / commitment, collaboration, innovation, employee growth and development, alignment, self-accountability

Figure 3. Inward and outward mindset in organizations[5]

As a corollary of requiring a complete vision and fundamental depth, digital transformation requires massive support from top management. Digital transformation cannot succeed as an isolated initiative of functional managers. We cannot interpret it as an implementation project for an information system. Software houses offer a wide range of solution with the potential to facilitate digital transformation in one functional area or another. They also offer platforms to support the transformation of a range of functions, including the integration for smooth operation. But without the behavioral change, we cannot realize the benefits of transformation.

Organizations, however, cannot achieve lasting fundamental behavioral change without a change in their mindset. A change so fundamental, in return, demands active involvement, support, and demonstration of leadership from top management.

Digital transformation is a cross-functional strategic initiative requiring a complete vision and demanding fundamental mindset change. It cannot succeed without dissolving the status quo and accepting the paradigm shift behind it.

Top management shall lead such a change. Transformation must involve leaders of all functions in the endeavor, as its core is re-engineering processes around redesigned business models. While we cannot reduce digital transformation to an information system implementation project or program, the Chief Information Officer of the organization has a specific role. We look closer at this role in the next chapter.

TOM ROZSAS

The role of IT

The information technology unit and the CIO of the organization are the owners of the digital transformation strategy and roadmap. This ownership goes beyond budgeting for IT operational and project expenses and executing system implementation projects.

The CIO should lead the transformation in a strategic sense. The digital transformation strategy should be among the pillars of the organization's strategy.

What does leading digital transformation in a strategic sense mean? Traditional IT is a provider of demanded technical services and a support function. As information systems evolved, IT has also become the specialist of information management.

Information is a strategic resource today. Organizations having an edge in information management also have an overall competitive advantage. IT has become a strategic function for its expertise and responsibility in information management.

In digital transformation, IT controls the agenda. It develops transformation strategy, harmonizes business initiatives, takes the lead and drives the process. To become a strategic leader, IT uses its experience in platforms, interdependencies, and synergies. In execution, IT controls the roadmap, determines the sequence of programs and projects based on dependencies, and communicates strategy to business partners. In its communication role, IT listens to business needs, explains technical constraints and potential, and influences strategic decisions in a consultative manner.

However, IT remains a support function. It must respond to business needs and serve the core mission of the organization. The CIO and IT managers need to have a business acumen and think about information strategy from a business perspective beyond their technical expertise. IT cannot dictate a digital transformation strategy. IT needs to persuade its business partners. Information management expertise, demonstrated understanding of the industry of the organization, its business goals and needs are the sources of its influence.

IT can only deliver if it develops expertise in business processes and business modeling and understands strategy formulation and strategic needs. To be strategic, IT must be able and willing to take this strategic role.

Strategic IT in return is the owner of information management strategy. In this role, IT drives the digital transformation strategy and roadmap. Strategic IT not only responds to emerging business needs but leads transformation.

Strategic IT creates needs where they should be and explains the roadmap where immature business initiatives would ignore dependencies. Communication is key in leading fundamental strategic change associated with digital transformation.

First, IT needs to listen to business partners to develop a thorough understanding. This is a process of discovery. IT explores potential benefits of transformation by keeping its stethoscope on the information flows of the organization.

Second, IT develops the transformation strategy in partnership with business functions, explains dependences, helps to compare alternatives, and manages expectations.

Business partners can help information strategy formulation by expressing their needs. They need to study industry best practices and develop expertise in their own fields so they can identify needs and professional development pathways.

When they look at benchmarks, they should strive to understand business models and processes instead of supporting technical solutions.

Business partners should communicate with IT and each other about needs, strategy, and roadmap. They should challenge a reactive IT to take a strategic role, but should not take initiatives in system implementation.

There is a catch in business taking the lead in system selection and implementation. Particular business functions may advance in their own transformation at the cost of further isolating themselves from the rest of the organization. When functions act as silos, the organization cannot transform. Processes may speed up within the silos, but slack will accumulate at organizational boundaries.

Business should demand IT taking a strategic role, but business functions cannot take the lead in digital transformation.

IT has a leading role in digital transformation based on its expertise in information management and modeling business processes. Business should challenge a reactive IT to fill this role but cannot take over.

Digital transformation is a cross functional endeavor involving fundamental changes in underlying structures. To understand the complexity of transformation, we inspect the depth of this endeavor in the next part.

THE SCOPE OF THE ENDEAVOUR

TOM ROZSAS

Technology enables transformation

In this second part, we unfold the layers of digital transformation. We decompose digital transformation and look at elements and conditions of a successful change.

We start with the role of technology in the first chapter. Technology enables digital transformation. New tools make fresh approaches possible, but in themselves they will not change how we work.

Digital transformation has been made possible by advances in computing and communication. Technology development pushed prices of information processing capacity and communication bandwidth down to a level that IT became pervasive. Complexity of IT systems also grown.

Today, we have computers in our pockets more powerful than server computers a few decades ago. They not only process data but play high definition video, track our location, and communicate with other machines over the internet from our bathroom scale to our car to our bank account. In the office, we have even more computing and communication power. The computing capacity of these tools are impressive. However, this is not their crucial characteristic. The real potential is in the fact that they are all connected. However, devices alone will not lead to change.

Folders in the cloud instead of your hard drive will not change the way you work. Employees virtuoso in registering to Facebook events are not yet the cutting edge of your labor force. If you implement new systems only to work faster, you may only build more slack.

Digital transformation is about the way we work, not the tools we use. Technical development adds new tools to our toolbox. With a wider selection of tools, we also have more ways to approach the same problem. It is like having more gears on our bike. We can be more efficient by always turning the pedals at our optimal cadence.

Some new tools are improved versions of old ones. Others have features and functions we did not have before. Pervasive computing and constant connection to the web are such novelties. Instead of performing our task and handing our output over when completed, we can now collaborate real time on the same object. This is not only about speed. Transparent, real time collaboration helps us harmonize individual contribution, reduces redundancy and waste, and helps us share knowledge. It also inspires to find new solutions.

To exploit this potential, we need to change the way we work and share information. Technology has the potential. But we need to adapt. The meticulous reconstruction of off-line access rights and approval pathways to protect management authority in a cloud base environment will not transform but paralyze the organization.

Technology can only help if we allow it. If we fall back to old default practices, we implement new systems in vain. We need not only change the way we work. We need to be active learners and change agents. Intellectual understanding of the benefits of novel approaches is not enough. For lasting change, we need to be vigilant guardians of our changed processes until they become our defaults.

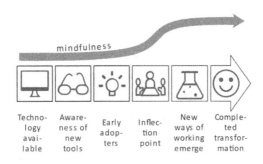

Figure 4. Stages of digital transformation

As you may see on the figure above, digital transformation is a long process of organizational learning. A precondition is availability of new technology. But the process only starts when people become aware of the new tools.

Early adopters will experiment with the new tools, but awareness needs to reach a critical level to start the transformation. This is what I call the inflection point. Discussions start in the organization about ways to exploit the potential of technology more effectively.

Fresh ways of work emerge from these discussions and find supporters. As people learn and adapt, the organization transforms. As the new methods engrave, the process completes.

Understanding the benefits and true adaptation are key to successful transformation and lasting results. Changes only last if people involved are mindful about the transformation and its benefits. We cannot trick or force people in the open ways of collaboration associated with the transformation.

Technology is a key component of digital transformation, but it is only an enabling factor. It is a catalyst, not an ingredient. Without technology, there is no transformation, but the change does not unfold in the computers.

The core of digital transformation is a change in our approach to collaboration. It is a paradigm shift. We discuss this fundamental change in the next chapter.

TOM ROZSAS

The paradigm shift

Technology enables fresh ways of work. Benefits depend on our use of this opportunity. Processes we develop to use technology are the core of the transformation.

In this chapter we go over the key elements of our novel approach to work. We start with a reminder of the achievements of the digital revolution. Then we review its consequences and affects on business processes.

Digital revolution had two parallel streams feeding from the same source: advancement in microelectronic technology. One stream was the rapid increase in computing power. The other is dynamic advancement in communication technology. With communication going digital, the two streams intertwined and reinforced each other.

Technical development also brought two further benefits. Size of components and equipment and prices dropped. Advances in communication technology made interconnectedness possible. Miniaturization and diminishing prices made computing pervasive.

Advancement in microelectronic technology also brought better and smaller sensors. Today, a common smartphone fitting in your pocket has sensors for motion, rotation, proximity, light, fingerprint, a compass, and radio receiver for navigation. Small and cheap sensors, processors, memory, and communication modules enabled the internet of things. We can now embed computers in many of our devices to collect, process, and forward data for central processing or use data in place for advanced control functions.

Beyond having a powerful computer in our pocket, our car, refrigerator, washing machine, even our light-bulbs are now connected. They can all collect data and we can control them or let them control themselves over the internet.

Pervasive computing changes how we cooperate. The change is not only about better ways of communication with others. Interconnectedness and pervasive computing enables the capture of information where it is created. Immediate share of information is also possible. As a result, everyone can rely on the same information even without direct communication between team members. This is not only about speed. By having a single source of truth and shared information, we can avoid many errors and mistakes. We can also correct remaining mistakes fast.

There is one important precondition, though. Technology only helps if we exploit its potential. If we set virtual barriers to recreate the physical ones we used to work with, we cannot transform.

During the first industrial revolution, we developed the functional organization. Back then, this facilitated efficiency by supporting the division of labor. As a side effect, silos emerged. Silos are self isolating units within the organization with a focus on their own responsibility instead of the success of the organization. Silos are also informal power centers. Once established, they protect themselves. One way of protection is to become a function within the organization who can block vital processes.

Silos are powerful. To exploit the potential of new technology, we need a flexible and transparent operation. Functions should become pools of expertize instead of silos. If parts of the organization are not willing to work in a transparent, cooperative way, transformation is not possible.

The precondition of successful digital transformation is transparent, open cooperation. Instead of dissecting business activities, we need well articulated models. Models that help us understand the business activity as a whole.

Why transformation is so hard? First, it challenges the status quo. Successful digital transformation eliminates the power base of silos. Second, transparent operations make errors visible. Being exposed to scrutiny, we may feel vulnerable. But we can also correct errors fast. Admitting and correcting our errors can be exercises in integrity.

Others will make mistakes too. When we help each other detect and correct mistakes for better results, we develop genuine teams.

The ultimate hallmarks of successful digital

transformation are cooperating teams instead of silos. Managers aspiring to transform their organization need to encourage open cooperation. Instead of rationing resources, they need to develop genuine teams. Their strive for contribution should replace protecting silos. Instead of supervising subordinates, they need to coach team mates and work on optimizing processes and eliminate obstacles.

So implementing a shiny new application is only the tip of the iceberg in digital transformation. Even teamwork and cooperation are above the waterline. What is below the waterline? We discuss it in the next chapters.

Figure 5. Digital transformation - the tip of the iceberg.

The basis of digital transformation is a paradigm shift. Outcomes of the digital revolution are only enable a better way to work. Transformation depends on our willingness to adapt.

Systems we implement and re-engineered processes are only the tip of the iceberg. Successful digital transformation requires more fundamental changes. We go below the waterline in the next chapters.

Replace your business model

To adopt novel ways to work, we need to look at our business activities from a fresh perspective. We cannot just do the same, but faster. But new methods need new models.

We often describe novel technologies disruptive referring to their potential to destroy existing industries by offering much better solutions. But technology itself is not disruptive. If we produce faster and cheaper, we may beat the competition and rearrange the market, but we cannot destroy an industry.

Disruption is not a workaround or an efficiency game. Disruption need a novel approach to a problem. If technology has disruptive potential, we need to have a new perspective to exploit it. Not technology, but our thinking has to be disruptive.

This is important because habits are hard to change. If we use disruptive technology in a traditional way, we may get faster, but that is not disruption. This is scaling at best. We invest and grow proportionally, a strategy easy to copy by competitors.

Growth by gradual improvements makes sense. It may bring lasting results and can keep us at the forefront of our industry. But it is not a transformation.

Acceleration of our processes without a profound revision and re-engineering may even have an adverse impact. Error prone, inefficient processes often rely on the human component to correct its mistakes. When steps of a poorly designed process are misaligned, but you work with experienced personnel, your processes may look smooth but slow. They may tempt you to automate to speed them up.

However, these processes look smooth because experienced personnel can correct mistakes on the go. Corrections slow down the process but keep it rolling. When you automate, you eliminate these informal corrections. They may look like redundant iterations to you, but these iterations keep operations running. If you eliminate them without changing the process, your operations will halt. You will need even more time and effort to keep the organization running.

Our traditional models rely on the functional division of labor. We cut our processes into steps with rigid boundaries and focus on a separate maximization of efficiency in each step. The approach comes from the industrial revolution.

For long, we had no better choice as we could not share information real time. Digital revolution allowed to shift the focus on overall efficiency. New models help us see how our part fits in the process. With shared information, we work with flexible boundaries. Instead of following instructions, we contribute.

The fresh approach helps us perform more complex activities. For example, we can design and build more complex products. This is the essence of digital transformation.

Look at project management as an example. Project managers no longer sit in an office commanding others around. Instead, they contribute by providing expertise in planning and problem solving. They remove obstacles from the team's path.

Digital revolution allowed project managers to provide better visibility. We can now use resource pools and adjust project cycles to level loads and eliminate bottlenecks in advance.

But technology only offers the opportunity. Instead of hardworking bureaucrats, we need project managers who understand project fundamentals and orchestrate complex cooperation of cross-functional teams. We also need project models that reveal the interplay of project elements.[6]

Another project management example is the spread of the agile approach. Agile is an excellent example because we can apply agile methods with no advanced IT support system.

The essence of agile is a radical interpretation of the project cycle. Agile takes the traditional project cycle, cuts it into small pieces, glues them back together, enabling rapid delivery of small increments instead of a single large delivery.

Agile relies on cross-functional teams of users and developers working in close cooperation. It integrates validation, development, and specification in an intense cycle delivering an increment.

Intense communication and close cooperation are at the core of the agile approach. While its power is in the model, advanced information systems and the internet extends its applicability. Advanced information systems combined with the agile approach revolutionized project management in the last decades.

A last example is new product development and product improvement. Product development is a complex process. From idea generation to project selection to product launch and aftermarket care, it requires the cooperation of all functions in the organization.

Digital transformation has tremendous potential in such a complex process. Contributors may all work from the same information. They inspire each other for better ideas and discover synergies. They trade crucial resources between competing project to maximize the value of the portfolio.

Share of information and communication is key in realizing the potential of digital transformation. An overarching model providing a framework for the common interpretation of this information, however, is not less important.

Development of new business models is a delicate task. The thorough analysis and careful design we need require time, expertise, and a deep understanding of our industry.

Fortunately, we are not alone. Professional organizations of our industry are likely to have the model we need already. In fact, leading software houses base the advanced IT solutions they offer on these models. The best strategy to start digital transformation is to study your industry models. Before you check the market for IT solutions, visit the website of the professional organizations of your industry. Study their standards, best practices, and models. Once you understand the conceptual models of your industry, you know what to look for in IT solutions and which of them meets your needs best.

On the surface, we may perceive digital transformation as implementing new information systems. For real transformation, we need to go further by changing the way we work. Share of information, close cooperation, and a shift from following instructions to a culture of contribution are key to success.

This new approach also needs new business models. Access to the same information is a necessary but not sufficient condition of successful digital transformation. We also need models to serve as frameworks for common interpretation.

Ripple effects

A model change has consequences. Our current processes work in a context. When we change the model, our processes change. We can only follow our changed processes if we also adjust the context.

This chapter is about the consequences of model change. The adjustments we need to make and the conditions of proper operation.

We acquired two important ingredients of successful transformation so far. We have technology, the enabler, and our model what makes the proper use of technology possible. If we have done our homework well, the IT systems we chose to implement combine technology and the right model.

But how can we use these components to our advantage? We need to learn; it is obvious. But there is a crucial step: we need to adapt. We can only take advantage of the models embedded in our systems if we use them, not fight against them.

Yes, we need to learn and adapt. Adaptation means we do not turn around the model to make it resemble our old ways of working. It means we accept the need for change and act on it.

To adapt, we must forget and let our routines go. This is very hard. Often, we invested years or even decades in our current routines. We may even base our influence in our organization on our expertise in current processes. It is hard to sacrifice our personal advantage for the interest of the organization.

We cannot insist on these advantages if want to succeed. We can only adopt a new model by re-engineering our processes around it. This is the reason we need to study models first and then select supporting IT solutions. The software is only style. One may prove more handy than the other, but they all do the job. We need to understand and adopt the model to succeed.

Processes, in return, define jobs and job requirements. The change is not about titles and paygrades but new roles and skill sets that fit them.

This is another crucial and difficult transition. We invested in our present skills, hoping to realize a return on our investment. Will are skills be valuable? If not, will we be compensated for acquiring new skills?

When we see our skills devalue, we perceive a threat. We believe it is unfair to give up our status for a change decided by others.

If we cannot get through these obstacles, transformation may not complete. We cannot bend job descriptions to favor team mates. But we must make the benefits of transformation clear and prove that we compensate everyone for their effort at the end.

Jobs define the skills we need. Some skills transfer well, others may devalue, and our team may lack some crucial ones. Expertise remains important, but we need better communication and cooperation skills in an environment based on open cooperation.

The ability to learn will be paramount. If people have objections to learning, it will be difficult. So we need to manage expectation well. We need to prepare people to feel challenged and struggle with new tools and processes first. We need to clarify that this is an unavoidable part of the transformation process, and it is not a sign of weakness but excellence.

Our attitude to and ability of learning remains important even beyond the transformation. Open cooperation relies on integrated models, platforms, and our understanding of our role. We also need to understand the roles and perspectives of our team mates so empathy is key.

To contribute, we often need to learn steps carried out by team mates to help. As we see the same shared information, we need to understand the model and our processes to know whom to tell when we detect an error. Instead of workarounds, we can correct mistakes and errors if we know where to intervene.

Openness also requires strong people skills. When others see how we approach and tackle a problem, we may feel vulnerable. By time, we realize everyone is busy with their own problems, so they may only look at our solutions for inspiration. But as systems get smarter and more autonomous, the emphasis shifts back from machines to people and human creativity. This human creativity is the ultimate resource of the organization. The eventual goal of the transformation is to expose this creativity to real problems instead of handling routine tasks fast.

A new model of our business activity has a ripple effect in the organization. We can only exploit the benefits of digital transformation if we adapt to the new models. Adaptation means we accept change and render our processes around the model. Then, we redefine jobs and required skill sets and launch a learning endeavor, shaking the status quo in all sense.

In our iceberg metaphor, this is under the waterline already but still close to the surface. In the next chapter, we go deeper.

The iceberg under the water

Digital transformation is a people change. Technology covers its outside layer, but it goes even deeper than processes, business models, and job descriptions.

Technology enables a more flexible and responsive way of cooperation, but we need to change our models and processes to exploit its potential. Why this change is difficult? Because we not simply reprogram machines to follow a different set of instructions. We transform people at the end.

When we understand the way an organization works, we often use the machine metaphor. The organization comprises components fitting together. We consider people a subset of these components or machine operators.

The four-frame model developed by Boleman and Deal to better understand organizations reveals a few more layers.[7] Four-frame model looks at organizations through four different frames: structural, HR, political, and symbolic.

Structural frame uses the machine or factory metaphor. It deals with rules, goals, policies, roles, technology, and environment. It captures the technical aspects of digital transformation, including the model and processes.

The metaphor of HR frame is the family. HR frame

deals with needs, skills, and relationships. It captures the HR aspects of digital transformation including job descriptions, skill sets, and employee development.

The political frame uses the jungle metaphor. It is about power, conflicts, competition, and organizational politics. We touched upon the political frame when I spoke about sources of influence or the status quo.

Through the fourth frame, we see the organization as a carnival, temple, or theater. This is the symbolic frame which is about meaning, culture, rituals, stories, and heroes.

The symbolic frame explains the deepest level of change. Change at this level is difficult not only because changing habits takes time. This is the level where beliefs and hidden assumptions also live. Without mindful attention, we may not even be aware of the motivations we have.

Organizational culture belongs to the symbolic frame. Culture provides meaning and incorporates our values. Values root deep in the organization, so culture is difficult to change. Digital transformation is a case when we need cultural change.

Digital transformation often takes place at highly optimized functional organizations at the forefront of their industry. They have a solid basis to grow and want to make a confident step forward.

Among their key characteristics are clear boundaries

of responsibility and a professional ethos. Members of these organizations are eager to do their job well, but they focus on their own domain of responsibility and expertise, not on common achievements.

An emerging strategic IT enters this environment with its agile approach, professionals often with certificates from leading tech companies replacing traditional college degrees, and alternative ideas about cooperation.

No wonder they meet resistance. Especially when they cannot or forget to explain that behind IT applications there are models developed by experts of the supported business activities.

Digital transformation can only succeed if it can soften these boundaries between functional units. Replacement of professional vanity with an emphasis on contribution to the organization's mission is the first pillar of transformation.

Expertise remains important. But we measure merit with the value of support to others and contribution. Instead of hoarding resources and claiming authority over their domain, functions need to give away expertise and resources to support each other. They need to seek for opportunities to help. They need to be empathic.

This outward looking culture is the foundation of the iceberg. The strength of the iceberg metaphor is its power to explain that the mass below the waterline provides all the lift.

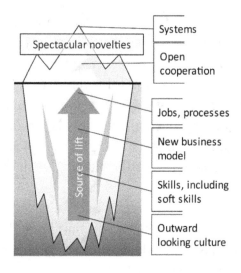

Figure 6. The iceberg below the waterline

Cultural change on the organizational level is a deep learning process and a change in attitudes on the individual level. Organizational culture is not an entity but a set of characteristics. When we speak about cultural change, we speak about people change.

Culture is a set of shared values, beliefs, and practices. To change organizational culture, we need to change people's attitudes and beliefs.

To create an outward looking culture, people need to be outward looking. Trust among members, empathy, and finding value in learning from each other provide thrust to digital transformation.

People are the ultimate resource of an organization. They are the vital components of systems and processes. The success of digital transformation also depends on people and their readiness to change.

While changing attitudes, values, soft skills are below the waterline, they provide all the lift to carry the weight of the spectacular part of digital transformation.

Dream big but

Digital transformation involves fundamental changes. Organizations setting off digital transformation should have bold goals. But digital transformation is not for every organization. Boldness of vision is a necessary but not sufficient condition for success.

In technical terms, the core of digital transformation is automation of routine processes to free human capacities for value creation. Automation of processes requires well-defined, logical processes and management willing to give up discretionary power. Exceptions are expensive and undermine the pursuit of automation.

Optimization and improvement of automatized processes also need a great deal of transparency. Processes should not be organized around personal preference, but overall efficiency.

We cannot automatize undefined, flimsy processes, ad hoc operation, and discretionary management decisions on individual cases. While best practice based model provide foundation to process definitions, organizational readiness also depends on management culture.

Software Engineering Institute of Carnegie Mellon University developed a framework to measure readiness and help process improvement. The Capability

Maturity Model Integration (CMMI) framework classifies organizations to five levels based on the maturity of their processes.[8] The figure below displays CMMI categories, I continue with their description below the figure.

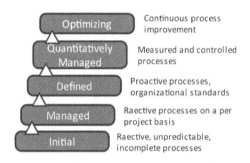

Figure 7. Levels of organizational maturity

Initial is the lowest level in the CMMI framework. Its denomination refers to the type of processes characteristic to the organization. On this level, the first processes emerge from the primordial soup of ad hoc operation.

Processes are reactive responses to repetitive situations. They are incomplete, belonging to corporate folklore rather than a formal set of rules. These processes often transmitted orally within the organization. On this stage we often hear the phrase "this is how we used to do it."

Managed is the next level of process maturity. This is

the stage where defined processes begin to take shape. Formal processes emerge, but still only in reaction to situations.

Processes defined on this level are not universal within the organization. Some projects use them, others may copy, but their use depends on ad hoc management decisions.

Managed level is important in organizational evolution. Awareness of the need for processes emerges here.

Defined is the level where organizational standards appear. When organizations realize the value of processes, they switch from reacting to emerging situation to expecting the need for processes and develop standards.

The importance of this level lies in the appearance of process integration. As standard processes emerge by design, we need to define interfaces and handover points between them. The emergence and understanding of interconnected processes is a precondition of successful digital transformation.

On quantitatively measured level, performance indicators to facilitate efficiency management appear. Organizations on this level are no longer satisfied with knowing how they operate. They want efficiency.

Measuring performance is not merely a supervision tool. It facilitates process improvement by exposing bottlenecks, non-value-added steps, and inefficient configuration. The insight gained from performance indicators is often a source of motivation for digital transformation.

Optimizing is the highest level of process maturity. Process optimization appears much earlier. It becomes an integral part of operations on this level.

On the optimizing level, we do not refine processes on an ad hoc basis, reacting to emerging situations. Optimization becomes the norm. Organizations incorporate it in their system of processes. In simple terms, organizations have formal processes for optimization on this highest level.

Organizations reach a level of maturity when their processes work as described on the particular level. You may have the most complex set of formal processes, your organizational maturity level cannot be high if you do not follow them. Members of the organization must know the processes. Managers should limit exceptions to extraordinary events.

What maturity level we need for successful digital transformation? An organization should reach at least defined level before it launches an initiative on digital transformation. As we can adopt models based on industry best practices, it seems possible to start digital transformation from a lower level. However, transformation is about people, not information systems or even processes. If management and members of organization have no experience in following formal processes, they will interfere with automatized processes and render them dysfunctional.

So be bold when you launch digital transformation. But start from the appropriate level. Patience pays. If you are below the defined level, work on stepping on the next level instead.

Digital transformation initiatives should be bold. We should expect significant results and fundamental change. But we need to be realistic. Organizations must reach at least defined level of process maturity before they can succeed with digital transformation.

Organizations striving for success but below defined level should work on reaching the next level of maturity instead.

Tom Rozsas

The transformation project

Once we understand that digital transformation is a people change and start from the right level, we are ready to go. Our next challenge is the fair navigation of the change process.

We will explore the management of transformation projects in the third part. The next chapter is an introduction to a typical transformation project to prepare us for the journey.

Digital transformation is a strategic initiative. We cannot transform the organization within a single project. We need a program sponsored by the CEO, coordinated by the CIO, governed by the board. Business champions, leaders passionate about change in their own fields, drive the process.

However, we need to start somewhere. We need to break down this endeavor into manageable chunks. We structure the program into projects so we can assign tasks and resources and start execution. Projects follow the same roadmap, but they are complete entities themselves. We discuss these projects in this chapter.

Why is it important to understand a single transformation project? We need to break down the program to projects to execute. Projects are key building blocks of the program. Besides, organizations often follow the alternative approach of starting with a single project and develop transformation strategy later.

We center each project around one business activity and one support system. If the CIO takes care of the roadmap, the key concern of business leaders will be the project, not the program. The right interpretation of transformation projects is even more crucial when CIOs ignore their responsibility for the roadmap and the transformation strategy.

The precondition of sound project definition in digital transformation is the recognition that we deal with a transformation project. Sponsors need to identify projects as business transformation project. Then they need to set goals and define scope considering the non-technical, business focus of transformation projects.

Transformation projects start with the understanding of the business model to be introduced during the process. You should have a model ready before selecting the IT solution of your choice. If you have none, or you do not have thorough knowledge about your model, start with a strong study phase.

Transformation projects are change projects. Change management has a crucial role in digital transformation. It is not only an integral part of the project. Change management activities must start well before the project and finish last.

In transition projects, change management is not a collateral subproject but the shell of the project. It prepares, leads, and drives the change. It is not just a tool to dampen resistance and offer aftercare to people affected.

The change manager in a transformation project is the business project manager. It is a change project. Project managers shall have a skilled change management expert in their staff, even if they are trained in change management themselves. A dedicated change management team may perform specific tasks, but the entire team handles change.

The figure below captures the relation of change management to other project elements.

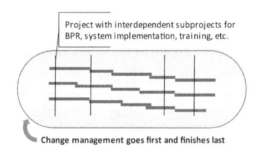

Figure 8. Change management encapsulates the transformation project.

Change management acts like a shell for the transformation project capsule. It goes first and finishes last. Change management mobilizes the organization well before the project initiation. It is also responsible for building and maintaining a guiding coalition for the change. After project completion, change management works on capturing lessons learned and incorporate them into organizational culture. It also works on making the changes stick.[9]

Inside the capsule, we find interdependent subprojects and work streams. Transformation projects are complex. They have components for business process re-engineering, IT system implementation, interface definition and development, and training. The project team also needs to support affected members of the organization. They need to look and listen for signs of misunderstanding, inertia, dissent, and opportunities. Who is in charge of a transformation project? Keep in mind that transformation projects are business projects. They have business goals and focus. Success is measured by business satisfaction and business results. Therefore, digital transformation projects shall have a business project manager. When the project involves an IT system implementation subproject complex enough, the project manager shall have an IT subproject lead or coordinator in their staff.

On the program or transformation strategy level, CIO or a dedicated senior program manager reporting to the CIO shall act as program manager. This program manager is responsible to handle interdependencies between projects. What matters more, the board shall govern the program with C-level executives acting as project sponsors for transformation projects in the areas of their responsibility.

Transformation projects entail sweeping change. High level support for the initiative is crucial for momentum.

Change management activities after project closure are crucial for lasting change. Transformation is not complete when we have systems implemented and users trained. Old habits live on. Inertia can still reset changes.

You need professional change management and strong business support to prevent the ball from rolling back from the hill. Formal training for new processes and systems is still part of the transformation project core. Measures to make sure changes last are line management responsibilities.

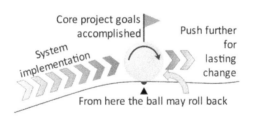

Figure 9. Active change management prevents
a reset after project completion

The building block of an organizational digital transformation strategy are transformation projects. Change management encapsulates the transformation project. It breaks the path at start and prevents the ball from rolling back at the end. Strong business project managers are best to lead transformation projects with direct support from IT. CIO shall coordinate on program level with the board governing the transformation program and strategy.

In the next part, we discuss the transformation project, the building block of the transformation strategy.

MANAGING TRANSFORMATIVE CHANGE

Scope

Realization of a digital transformation strategy is the execution of a chain of transformative change projects. To succeed in our strategy, we need to define the right projects and then execute them well.

When we define scope, we think in two dimensions. We think in span and depth. Span is the subject and extent of our scope. It is about what we include, what we need to care about. Depth is about how deep we dig, what foundation we build.

Projects in a digital transformation strategy are transformative change projects. I keep repeating this because this defines their scope.

Transformative change projects differ from system implementation projects. In a system implementation project, we have a structured problem with a fixed scope. System implementation projects have a technical focus and a limited learning component.

Example is a version upgrade of an existing system. Users will work with the same conceptual model, the new version brings only marginal functional changes and probably some additional comfort or efficiency.

Another example is implementing general purpose systems supporting business activities. Again, users will work the same way, they only get tools for specific tasks they perform. Single tasks may be more comfortable or efficient to perform, but the conceptual framework does not change.

In transformative change projects, the focus is on the conceptual change. Implementing a new system is only a consequence of the fundamental change.

To define a change project right, we must understand change. Change has countless models grasping and emphasizing one aspect or other. I introduce two of the most simple here to set the frame.

The five-phase model breaks the change process in five phases. First, we identify the need for change. In an organizational setting, this means management sees a gap between actual performance and a desired state or perceived opportunity. Second, the change agent builds a lead team. The change agent can be a leader starting the change, a champion, or a professional change manager hired to navigate through the process.[10] The third step is designing the change process. In this phase, the lead team considers desired output, preconditions, resources, affects, possible unintended consequences, dissent, and inertia among others. Then they select the approach and start planning the process. They announce the change only in the fourth phase. The last fifth phase is the implementation.

The power of this model lies in its emphasis on preparation. Another model I want to show is the three-stage model of William Bridges.[11] The model is deceivingly simple. Its three phases are ending, neutral zone, and new beginning. The model resembles the un-freeze, change, freeze model of Kurt Lewin. I show it because of its powerful message that for something new to begin; we need to leave some old solutions behind.

Change and its implications determine the span of project scope. Transformative change projects are about people, individual and group learning, cultural change, new conceptual frameworks, enabling technology, and support systems.

Span of scope includes the business process re-engineering, change management, organizational learning, training, system implementation, transition, and data migration.

System implementation is a technical subproject. It may include adjustments on the infrastructure, hardware and software implementation, building interfaces to other systems, and training for users and operating personnel. System configuration and customization are often also parts of the system implementation subproject.

The focus of a transformative change project is on the business aspects. The support system often incorporates the logic of the conceptual business framework. This may cause the illusion that system implementation, especially system configuration drives the process. This is only true when business process re-engineering lags system implementation or missing. But omitting business process re-engineering and change management slows system implementation and makes is very hard. For a successful transformation, we must do all the work. If we do not plan for change management and business process re-engineering, they will be a hidden burden on system implementation. Ignoring them in planning will slow or halt the project.

Depth is the completeness and rigor of project scope. Implications of change also determine the depth required. Transformative change projects need to be meticulous and complete because we want lasting change. Organizational learning is a complex and delicate process. A change project does not end with training and testing the results of an implementation. Genuine change starts where the project ends.

When we define the depths of scope, we need to consider what we know and what we should know. Do we have thorough knowledge of business models and conceptual framework? Are we familiar with industry best practices? What do we know about the underlying models our selected system is built on?

A study phase and exploration of concepts, models, and best practices should precede the transformation project in the program. If the program did not have a study phase, we should add it to the project or start with a study project instead.

If we have already gained knowledge of concepts, models, and practices, we need a preparation phase to design the change process. Only then we can start a complex implementation phase including business model adoption, system implementation, and training. The last phase is a change focused aftercare period to make sure changes last.

Implications of change are the key factors in the definition of transformative change projects. We need to manage both span and depth of scope to succeed. Digital transformation projects have a technical component, but their focus is on people, business models, and change.

Beyond scope, positioning of transformative change projects is also important. We discuss this in the next chapter.

Level

Besides scope, position in the organization's portfolio also affects success of a digital transformation project. Transformation involves cultural change and affects business activities next to our starting point. Therefore, we need more than a single project to transform an organization. We start somewhere, but we need a program of interrelated projects to finish.

Changes in transformation are fundamental. Deep changes in organizations need strong executive support. Transformation projects are strategic or destined to fail.

So digital transformation is a strategic initiative. What does this mean? First, we cannot transform with below the radar, low budget stealth projects. The initiative and all projects on the roadmap must have clear champions and committed executive support.

Second, the CIO must be engaged in setting direction and driving progress. Once business leaders recognize the benefits of transformation and initiate the change, the CIO needs to take the lead. To explore solutions, clarify interdependencies, demonstrate integrated platform benefits, generate and analyze alternative paths are all CIO responsibilities.

Third, transformation champions must build a winning coalition. They must engage stakeholders, convince skeptical leaders, and make stakes clear. It is key to share the story with members of the organization. Leaders should tell them what is, and what could be.

Transformation projects are strategic because they involve cultural change. No organization can survive with two cultures, so transformation cannot be partial or it will not last.

When culture changes, it destabilizes the organization. We cannot change without this creative destruction. So destabilization is not a problem until we stop. But incomplete transformation either rolls back or leads to chaos. Repeat the cycle and CHAOS becomes an acronym in your organization. An acronym for CEO/CIO has another outstanding solution.

I you do not treat transformation as a strategic initiative, if you downplay transformation projects, you end up with failed projects and undermined credibility in change. When members see that their organization tries but cannot change, they may lose faith in its future.

There are different ways to start digital transformation. Top-down approach starts with a strategy and a roadmap. The initiative becomes a formal program in the organizational portfolio with a governing body, sponsor, program manager, plans, and all the bells and whistles of programs in the organizational portfolio.

Often, transformation starts in a corner of the

organization with a strong case and ambitions and competent team. If this limited transformation project addresses an important pain point of the organization, it may gain momentum and act like a snowball triggering an avalanche. But the case must be strong enough to activate and maintain committed top level support throughout the project and beyond.

So we can start transformation with distinct cases also serving as learning opportunities. But we need committed executive support and develop a full fledged digital transformation strategy later down the road.

We can start digital transformation in various ways, but there is only one way to end it: total transformation. Partial transformation will not last.

When you transform one business activity, but you stop, you create an efficient island in the organization equipped with better tools. An efficient island in a traditional sea cannot contribute to overall results. It completes its tasks fast and waits for others. The only way to realize some benefit from such an island is making it lean enough to other units being able to keep pace.

How you make a unit lean? You reduce its headcount. A more efficient unit will cope with its tasks with a smaller headcount, and you eliminate slack, but there are consequences. With this solution, you punish your best team for their achievement and send a powerful negative message to the entire organization. So your only option is to go forward until you transform the entire organization.

Digital transformation belongs to the strategic level in a project portfolio. Once we start transformation, we cannot stop before transforming the entire organization. The process is complex and fundamental. It requires committed support from top management and the mobilization of the entire organization.

Change is a crucial component of this strategic endeavor. We look at managing change in the next chapter.

Managing change

Change is the core of digital transformation. Change management is essential for its success. In this chapter, I review aspects of change that need attention from leaders of digital transformation projects.

Change management addresses the human aspects of transformation. It helps to understand goals, supports learning, builds trust, and channels feedback. It makes sure systems implemented will also be used for the benefit of the organization.

Unlike technical systems, we cannot implement change by setting up a new model and turning a switch. People understand, learn, develop new skills, and practice during the change. This takes time and effort. It also pushes them out of their comfort zone.

Change management must take the lead a go ahead of the project. Project manager and leaders must understand change before they can navigate for success. Change management must prepare people affected.

When people understand benefits and prepared for the inconvenience of learning in advanced, the project meets less perceived resistance. When leaders understand the change process, they do not take inertia and confusion as resistance.

The first task of change management is to raise awareness of the complexity of change. The figure below introduces four approaches to change and also shows they are interrelated.

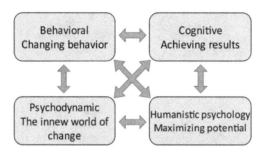

Figure 10. Aspects of change.

In digital transformation, we aim for results. This is the cognitive aspect. But we cannot achieve results without addressing other aspects as well. People need to change their behavior to learn, develop new routines, and let old ones go. Behavioral change, in return, relates to psychological comfort and motivation. Project managers need change management support to address these aspects.

Change affects people, and they respond to it. This response follows a typical pattern and time course captured on the figure below.

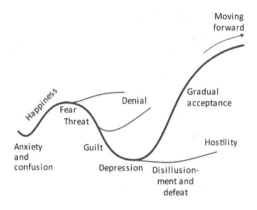

Figure 11. Individual response to change - the Fisher curve.

The Fisher curve above is a sophisticated version of the Kübler-Ross curve. I like to use it here because it reveals the traps of the change process.

As change pushes us out of our comfort zones, we respond with feeling confused and uncomfortable. Once we understand the stakes and see benefits, we get excited and eager to go on until complexity hits. As we face challenges, we may doubt we can succeed, but we also find solutions down the road and succeed.

The main curve captures this rollercoaster. But the change process may get derailed as indicated by the forks from this main curve. We may end up with a partial solution: taking an easy exit, or fail.

The rollercoaster relates to learning. We can replace machines and software. But when change involves people, learning is key.

Transformation requires people to learn new skills and develop new routines. But what they should not do is just as important. Often, the need to release established routines blocks the way of learning.

We need to go through several steps to change our routines and habits. We need to forget, learn, and practice to replace established routines with new ones. The figure below summarizes this process.

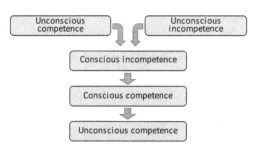

Figure 12. The individual learning process.

When we change how we work, we start with noticing our limitations. Our daily work relies on routines we practiced over the years and follow unconsciously. This is our unconscious competence. We are competent to the level we need not pay much attention to routine tasks.

If these routines work, we need not think about other ways of doing things. As a result, we are not aware of our lack of skills. We need not care. This is unconscious incompetence. This is our blind spot.

When we change the way we work, we realize we lack skills and knowledge, and what we know well works no more. In this first phase of learning, we face our limitations and recognize the need to learn. We notice our incompetence.

In the second phase, we gain new skills and knowledge. We become competent again. But we need to pay attention to routine tasks until we practice enough to develop new schemes in our mind. Once we practiced enough, we regain our unconscious competence in the new setup. We develop new routines. If we want lasting change, we need to go through all these phases.

So far, we spoke about change at an individual level. Organizational change results from individual changes and organizational learning. This adds a second layer of complexity.

Beyond learning the skills to do their job, people also need to learn the new configuration. In addition, they take part in the interactive shaping of this new configuration.

When we navigate change on an organizational level, we need to address individual differences, interdependencies, conflicts, and other variables related to human interactions. The Carnall model shown on the figure below captures this complexity.

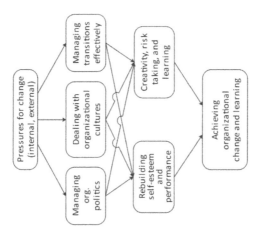

Figure 13. Organizational layer of complexity - the Carnall model.

Change management handles all aspects captured in the model. The change manager needs to deal with organizational politics to secure vital support. Culture is also important. Culture takes time to change, but change cannot last until culture and the fresh ways of operation are in harmony. Change management also needs to take care of the transition process. Facilitation of learning on individual and organizational level is a change management responsibility.

We need to cover all three bases to succeed in the creative, external part of change and in the internal, human part alike. Change cannot last if we develop poor solutions. But rebuilding self-esteem through improved performance is also necessary. We reach our goals in change only when we have both new solutions and unconscious competence in the new context.

Organizations can outsource system implementations and software configurations. But learning is internal. We cannot buy new skills. We may buy books, training materials, and hire experienced trainers, but we still need effort. So change management must take the lead in the transformation process.

How can change management lead? It should take the initiative in every stage and navigate the organization through the complexity of change.

The first step is to explain what the change is about. Show the benefits and show what can the organization lose by not taking the opportunity. Build a pressure of urgency around meaningful, significant story.

Then we need to build a winning coalition of evangelists, leaders, and experts supporting the case. Members of this coalition shape the vision and develop a strategy for change. This is the point where we mobilize the rest of the organization. We communicate the story, vision, and strategy. We persuade people to join and support the case.

The next step is to move in the envisioned direction. This phase is where transformation projects kick in. Once we start action, we achieve results and face challenges. Celebrate achievements and learn from failures. Celebrate milestones and closures of projects. But do not be overconfident. Transformation does not end when system implementation projects and trainings complete. Change management needs to track the evolution of cultural changes and make sure culture develops and changes last.

Change management is essential for successful transformation. Like a captain of a ship, the change manager boards first and leaves last. Change management focuses on the learning process at individual and organizational level. It deals with the complexity of individual learning and its psychological aspects, and organizational learning and its interference with the technical aspects of transformation.

Successful transformation is impossible without dealing with the human aspects of change. But we also need a plan. We look at the program structure of digital transformation in the next chapter.

Program structure

Digital transformation is a strategic initiative, a complex process. It cannot happen by chance and cannot emerge from small, independent IT projects. We want digital transformation to be a pillar of our deliberate strategy. So we need a plan. This chapter is about the plan.

As a major initiative of our deliberate strategy, we execute digital transformation as a program in the organization's portfolio. It is a complex program affecting core capabilities of the organization. Therefore, we need careful planning.

The program starts with exploration, learning, and planning. Before planning all further steps, we need to know our organization, our goals, and the basics of the models we can use. We need to map information flows in our organization so we can explore opportunities and dependencies. We need to learn about models and best practices to set the right goals. Also, we need to map the information flows we envision in our transformed organization.

The next step is developing a roadmap and establishing a governance structure. These structures hold our transformation endeavor together and handle project interdependencies.

Discovery of new models and solutions, learning

about industry best practices, and figuring out novel solutions to maintain a competitive edge are key to successful digital transformation. How can we navigate the exploration from the start to the end of our journey? How can we traverse on uncharted terrain? We can borrow an approach from new product development where we often face similar challenges.

The model we use as inspiration serves as a tool to manage risk arising from uncertainty in new product development. It splits the project to stages separated by gates where we review our achievements and challenges and decide to proceed, repeat the last stage, or kill the project. The figure below displays an overview of the stage-gate model with an adaptation to transformation projects.

Idea-to-Launch Stage-Gate System for New Product Development

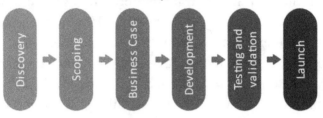

Stage-Gate inspired project cycle for digital transformation projects

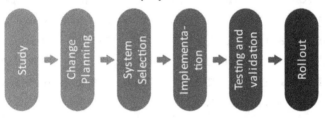

Figure 14. Managing risk and uncertainty in transformation - a stage-gate inspired approach.

The stage-gate model is based on an approach of taking only smaller risks until we have more information to avoid heavy losses. The figure above shows typical stages in new product development and stages for transformation projects. We can also apply the concept to the entire digital transformation program. The key component is the study phase at project or program start and the careful progression to the next stage.

The philosophy behind stage-gate us avoid costly mistakes. If we follow its gradual approach, we may start slow but finish fast. We can avoid detours and dismantling and rebuilding systems we configured wrong at the first time.

Parallel to study and exploration, we need to map the information flows of the organization. This is an important step at the start of the program.

Look at digital transformation as a journey. To traverse from one place to another, you need to know where those places are. Mapping the flow of information in your organization is defining the starting point of your journey.

The destination is not less important. Even though we cannot have all information, we also need to map the desired flow of information as best as we can.

The best approach to map information flows is starting with an enterprise architecture diagram. These diagrams capture the framework of our organization in various layers. The top layer is business architecture, further layers are information, applications, and technology.

Once we established our point of departure and destination, we need a plan to tackle obstacles on the way and make sure our resources last for the journey. We need a roadmap.

The roadmap is more than a simple high-level program cycle. Based on the maps of information flows, it captures key projects in their context and with their dependencies. While it is high level, it should be complete. All projects should be on the roadmap including study and planning projects for program planning, governance, and coordination. Change management on program and project levels should also appear on the roadmap.

Program level planning is preceded with a study phase. Its purpose is to explore opportunities, models, and best practices enabling us to utilize advanced digital solutions in business areas involved. We should also consider program level oversight and coordination a separate project. While governance and program level coordination are management activities, handling them in a project framework ensures they are not ignored and helps prevent problems. The figure below displays a schematic roadmap.

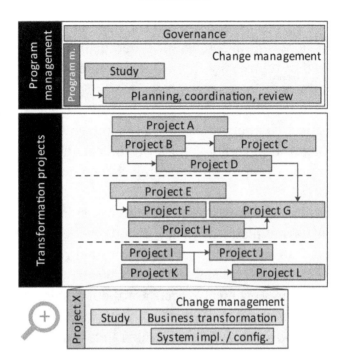

Figure 15. Digital transformation roadmap.

Structure of individual transformation projects also portrayed on the figure. Each project may have a study phase to explore business models and best practices related to the business activity affected. It helps to identify and prioritize business needs and establish an understanding of these models before system selection.

We can identify project dependencies from the information flow map. They follow dependencies between systems affected or to be implemented. Beyond simple project sequences, we can find interdependencies between milestones of different projects as affected systems may interact each other at multiple points.

Digital transformation projects always have a strong business component and a system implementation or configuration component. All technical and business components are embedded in a change management context.

Business subprojects are about transition to new models and platforms. They include modeling activities, change, training, review of internal regulations, workflows and processes, reconfiguration of the organization. Technical aspects are about system implementations and configuration, data migration, data flows and processes, technical training, and system adoption.

Governance is a key component of digital transformation programs. Digital transformation must be a high-level strategic initiative, not an emerging strategy taking shape from independent projects by chance.

Planning and program management should be one ongoing project on the roadmap. Why not just a regular ongoing management activity? Planning, review, and corrections should not be ignored. Having a planning project on the roadmap ensures continuous management support and attention.

The program planning and governance project also

has a project organization and a project manager responsible for maintaining the roadmap, starting projects, capturing lessons learned. Its project organization also acts as a professional planning and advisory staff for the program preparing high level management decisions.

If the organization is large enough, its digital transformation initiative may also deserve its own project management office.

Program planning starts with defining the points of departure and destination by mapping information flows. Then we need to establish a roadmap and provide resources and a governance structure.

We will discuss governance in the last chapter. Before we do that, I want to drop a few words on agile, a buzzword often misunderstood in the digital transformation context.

A word on agile

Agile is trendy and has been spreading fast in the software industry in the past decades, spilling over to other industries as well. But agile is often misunderstood. One sign of the vagueness of the term is the fact that we use the word agile alone. But when agile is an adjective. So when we say agile, we should pause for a moment and ask ourselves what we mean. Agile what? We may use agile in two senses in a digital transformation context. In the narrow sense, we may think of agile software development. In the broader sense, we may think of agile approach to projects in general.

Agile is trendy for a reason. Used well, the agile approach is an efficient tool for quick start, fast track projects. But you must know what you do so this chapter provides some reality check on agile.[12]

Its evangelists sell the agile approach with the label of quick start, steady delivery, and little overhead. They also say agile has an advantage when you do not have all details at the start but need results fast. Most of what they tell about agile is true. Part of what we hear is not.

True, we can start a project with agile approach without a detailed specification. Agile methods provide the means to develop detailed requirements as we go. But we still need to know what we want. We must have clear goals and an overall roadmap in our mind. We also need to be confident that we know our field well enough to develop detailed requirements as we go. Agile may work on uncharted terrain, but no method can guarantee results if you do not know what you want and what you are doing.

True, agile methods help us deliver fast and steady. But it does not mean they deliver the full scope. Agile deliveries are increments, starting with a few key functions, and add to them at each release. Early deliveries are good for feedback, exploration, and risk management. Having a system with full functionality takes time.

True, the agile approach is lightweight in terms of documentation overhead. But it does not mean you need not document what you do. In most cases, we have the same depth and detail with agile documentation only in a different structure. Instead of collecting requirements in one document, functional description in another and testing in a third, we break down the full documentation into user stories, and then add functional and test documentation to the user story. In addition, this works well only if we access and use the tools developed for the agile approach. While managing agile documentation in spreadsheets and word processors is possible, it is painful and prone to errors.

So the agile approach has great potential, but it is not a panacea or a simple escape. As there is no royal way to mathematics, there is no royal way to software development, system implementation, or business transformation. Agile promises fast start, steady delivery, and fast progress without asking the customer to come up with full specification at the start. But agile projects are intense endeavors requiring active participation and full commitment from the customer during the entire project.

In a sense, agile precedes all other approaches to project management. People completed significant projects well before they could come up with any defined and structured method for project management. At first sight, agile seems to be a denial of structured methods. The agile vs. waterfall comparison appears as a dichotomy of project management approaches. Supporters of the agile approach often portray structured models as outdated, rigid methods applicable only to simple missions.

Nothing is further from the truth. The choice between agile and structured project management is not a choice between two options but seeking the optimum on a wide adaptive-structured spectrum. Change is possible in a structured project. We can also manage uncertainty by defining stages, study phases, or adding iterations. In fact, we may also consider agile as a structured project where we took iterations to the extreme.

There is more than one dimension in selecting the right approach to our project. The Agile Practical

Guide introduces four project cycle categories along two dimensions. The first dimension measures change, the second the frequency of delivery. The four life-cycle categories are predictive, agile, iterative and incremental and the guide emphasizes the continuous spectrum between predictive and agile extremes.

According to the guide, predictive methods work best with low frequency of delivery and few changes. Agile methods fit projects where changes and delivery are frequent. Projects with lots of changes but few deliveries are iterative, projects with frequent deliveries but few changes are incremental.[13]

This is a more accurate view but leaves out risk from the calculations. High-risk projects with life and death consequences call for structured methods. In these cases, we handle uncertainties with study and experimental phases in a controlled manner. Last but not least, we may also combine agile and structured elements in the same project.

So never choose agile only to avoid developing a specification. Chose agile for a valid reason. Before we can work with the agile approach, we need to understand it. Go agile only when you know what you are doing. If you go agile without knowing its limitations and adopting its principles, do not blame the method for failure.[14]

The choice is complex but we can boil down the complexity to what we fix and what varies in a typical agile and structured setting. The figure below shows the difference and its key consequence.

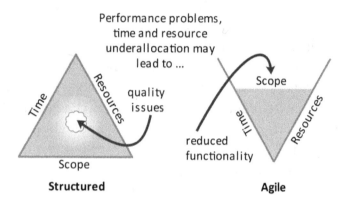

Figure 16. Agile vs. Structured advantages and drawbacks.

Structured projects have a fixed scope. We calculate what resources and time we need to cover the scope and adjust them when we need it. In agile projects, we do not start with a defined scope. We may have a general understanding of what we want, but no detailed scope definition. We have fixed time and resources and build our solution in small chunks.

The iron triangle of project management says the balance of scope, time, and resources defines the quality of our project execution. For a large scope, we need more time and resources. While there are trade-offs between time and resources, extremes are less efficient than a balanced mix. Structured and agile projects differ when we face a challenge, and our progress slows. In structured project, our fixed scope leads to quality problems when we under-allocate time or resources. In agile projects, quality does not suffer, but we realize a smaller scope. This is a choice between fewer bugs or fewer features in software development.

As agile works with a variable scope, transformation projects cannot follow the agile path. We can introduce agile components for system customization, for example, but adoption of a new business model calls for a fixed scope.

Once we have our business framework, developed a clear roadmap, and have a product owner to lead the project, we can rely on agile sprints for system configuration. But be prepared to add sprints to cover the entire scope if progress is slower than expected.

One more word of caution on agile is still needed. If our organization has no experience with the agile approach, introducing agile is a major change itself. This means, we need a change project to introduce agile in the organization.

The agile approach is flexible. We can use our own playbook and develop our own rules. But creating our own methods needs experience and careful thought. If your organization is new to agile, chose a well established method first and spend some time learning.

We not only have a wide selection of project cycles on the adaptive-structured spectrum. We may also mix agile and structured elements within a project. Agile and structured stages may alternate, or we may start with developing a detailed specification, go agile for software development, and return to the structured approach for rigorous testing. Our choice is endless.

But mixing approaches is an advanced level of project management. To succeed, we need to know both worlds well. Transformation projects are about complex change in unchartered terrain. Not knowing our navigation tools is dangerous in this setting.

Maybe the most important warning about agile is that we should not choose agile to avoid something. Agile is not about ignoring planning or documentation but putting them to the service of creating value. We do not ignore exploration and definition of requirements in an agile project but do it in small chunks. This is an intense process.

When we are vague with needs definition to save the effort, we do not follow agile principles, but do something else. We can compare agile projects to traversing a dense forest. We understand the forest and know our general direction, but we cannot figure out all of our steps in advance. Yet, we can traverse fast if we pay attention. But if we don't we keep bumping into treed. Going agile to avoid developing a clear specification while rejecting the intensity of the agile approach is not a different version of agile. It is a suicide run. We should not confuse the agile approach with the suicide run.[15]

The agile approach promises fast start and early delivery. It does not promise n effortless start and quick delivery of the entire scope. Agile is not a way to escape the rigor of a structured project. It is an approach to provide teams with flexibility and trading a long preparation phase for intense participation during the entire journey.

If you found this chapter full of cliché, agile may be right for you. You know the agile approach well. If it was disturbing, be careful. You can always hire experienced scrum masters, product owners, and agile coaches to support your team.

The last chapter coming next is our capstone chapter. Governance of projects looks simple. Instead of complex technical details, it is about setting direction and maintaining momentum. But good governance requires an understanding of the complete structure. We cannot make sound decisions without understanding the consequences.

Managing digital transformation

Digital transformation is a fundamental change affecting and involving the entire organization. Success depends coordinated effort of functions, units, and individuals involved. We need to focus on details without losing the big picture.

Coordinated effort needs sound management on project level, and good governance on program and strategic level. We cannot expect people working on details to keep direction and momentum without someone responsible for the vision.

This chapter discusses program governance, its structure, responsibilities, and its importance.

Strategic programs involve members of multiple units even on the project level and below. Their complexity and extension requires multi level management structure matching the breakdown of the program.

The program comprises projects, so the mid-tier of program management is project management. Transformation projects are complex themselves, so we need all the bells and whistles of a professional project organization. Depending on the approach you choose for the particular project, its organization can follow agile or structured principles with a product owner or project manager being in charge. Most likely, you need a project manager for two reasons. First, pure agile transformation project is viable in a program context but rare. Second, even when the technical project component calls for the agile approach, change management needs attention beyond the focus of the product manager.

Above project management, we need program management and governance levels. Program management handles program planning, coordination, tracking, and review. Governance handles top level support, removing obstacles and resolving conflicts, and decisions on direction and policies.

We often need to break down projects to subprojects or work streams with dedicated leads responsible for their progress. Delegation and empowerment are key on all levels, transformation projects are too complex for micromanagement.

Program management organization structure follows the levels of leadership. As a strategic initiative affecting the entire organization, digital transformation needs a governing body. This governing board comprises leaders of affected business areas, including IT. A dedicated program manager handles program planning and providing business expertise and advisory capacity for the program relying on a small permanent staff. The CIO of the organization also must be involved in providing expertise on technical issues and interdependencies. The CIO draws on the expertise of the IT department. For large organizations, dedicating a small IT staff to digital transformation is always a good idea.

Transformation projects of the program have their own project managers and project organizations. Depending on project size and complexity, project managers may also need a small, permanent staff.

The figure below shows an overview of the digital transformation leadership structure.

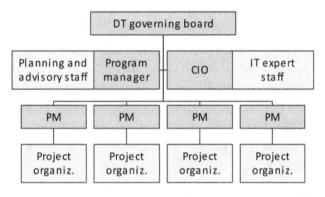

Figure 17. Governance structure of a digital transformation program.

The figure is a reminder rather than a detailed description. The multi-level structure reinforced with professional planning and expert staffs and a governing board are key.

Projects in a digital transformation program are still large and complex themselves. They need to address business, technical, and change aspects, breaking the mission down to subprojects and task blocks. Project managers must be able to delegate responsibility for subproject to senior team members or junior project managers.

Project managers also benefit from a professional staff, which is essential for large and complex transformation projects. The staff plans, tracks progress, reviews plans and outcomes, and support decisions. They support the project manager, subproject leads, and team members alike.

The staff is not a simple pool of administrative capacity. Staff members provide expertise in project and change management, business management, business models, and practices of the particular field. Staff members must be subject experts, project and change management experts, or both.

Planning is essential to the cooperation needed for successful transformation. Plans may change as teams react to changing circumstances but we cannot execute complex projects and programs without a sound roadmap and a having a scenario in advance.

Program level planning provides the structural framework. It follows a top-down approach, sets direction and breaks the mission down to projects and key milestones. The goal is to identify and manage dependences without restricting project managers.

Effort and resource estimates are bottom-up because effort estimation is more reliable for the small, routine activities building up the projects. Sound effort estimation is key because the plans must be realistic. If you plan with slack, your cost goes up and you lose momentum. If you plan for best case, you have two options. You may allocate hefty reserves to the projects or muddle through with continuous improvisation. A best case plan with hefty reserves equals to planning with slack. A best case plan with no reserves is suicide and constant struggle.

The best option is realistic planning with readiness to adjust plans when needed.

The staff of the program or project manager provides visibility for the complete team. It tracks progress, adjusts plans, and communicates status and modifications. The staff also develops scenarios for risk management and analyzes options to support decisions.

Maintenance of plans is an ongoing activity. Updates and changes are frequent. But despite the frequent changes, program and project plans have a key role in keeping momentum, working towards set goals, and avoiding scope creep.

Plans must include change management activities. Remember: change management is our first and last activity in a transformation project. We need to prepare the people affected by the change to avoid resistance. We also need to prepare team leads and team members to differentiate between inertia and resistant. Inertia always accompanies complex change. If you interpret it as resistance, you raise the resistance you imagined.

Change management is also the last activity. Transformation projects do not end when we have the new systems implemented and users trained. Transformation completes when novel ways to work become routine.

Communication is also an integral part of planning. Plans should include communication activities and plans should be communicated. Project and program visibility are key for execution and decision making.

Leads and staff should disseminate plans, progress, and results to team and stakeholders alike. They also need to look and listen. Thus they can appraise the effects of their efforts on the organization, detect problems early, react on time, and show empathy to dismantle emerging resistance.

Management of digital transformation is a complex, large scale effort itself. Leaders must be able to plan and coordinate on multiple levels. Delegate, empower, and motivate. Take the lead, and listen to their environment at the same time. Digital transformation is a strategic initiative. It must get the attention and support it deserves. Professional management, supported by a professional staff, is essential for success.

———————

Epilogue

Even if we accept the importance of digital transformation, is not this too much? Do I exaggerate or expect a level of attention impossible to provide in practice? After all, we do not drive digital transformation in a vacuum. Leaders and members of the organization also have other priorities. There is always a time pressure. People may lack experience. Can we complete digital transformation right at all? What if we cannot do it right?

Well, it will be slow and expensive. We will need several iterations to get the same results. Shortcuts and quick savings always have a heavy toll in complex programs like digital transformation. But we can do it.

If we have strong motivation and stamina, a trial-and-error approach may work. True, we will not get the same results. We are likely to exceed budget and miss deadlines. We will have detours and we will end up redoing work to get it right the second or third time. But it still worth it.

Remember, digital transformation is not about technology. It is about people, learning, and new ways of cooperation enabled by technology. So the most important aspect of digital transformation lies in its organizational learning potential. Even if we take the inefficient path, we learn during the process. If we persevere, we develop an experienced team which gets familiar with change and sees things in a different way.

Even our detours may be sources of innovation. While adopting industry best practice is a safe and efficient way to go, wandering into uncharted territory may bring new exploration.

But be careful. Do not expect these discoveries to make up for your inefficiencies. An indisputable gain of the trial an error approach, however, is lessons learned from these inefficiencies. Starting with transformation project the wrong way will help you understand why we need so much consideration.

Besides, perceiving digital transformation a messy process does not mean you are not doing it right. Learning is messy. Transformation is messy. We leave a familiar environment to implement models and processes we not yet understand. It is natural to feel insecure in the middle of transformation.

You may still not believe digital transformation deserves the elevated support from top management I am arguing for. Then consider this. Digital transformation focuses on people and new business models and processes introduced and implemented. It affects the entire organization. It transforms the way the organization operates. Digital transformation is not a technology project, it is a complete overhaul of how your organization works.

When you start such an overhaul, it is not a support

function in your strategic portfolio. It is the backbone of your strategy. The process that propels your organization into its future.

Notes

[1] The Magic Quadrant is a graphic classification of IT solution providers in various markets. It is maintained by Gartner, a leading technology and management consulting firm.

[2] A Google Trends search for the term shows the phrase only started to spread from early 2014.

[3] Read more on how the value chain helps us understand organizational capabilities in Grant, Robert M. 2002. Contemporary strategy analysis: Concepts, techniques, applications. 4th ed. Oxford: Blackwell.

[4] Arbinger Institute is a management think tank focusing on human cooperation in an organizational setting. Its website is available at https://arbinger.com

[5] Replacing the inward mindset with an outward mindset as the basis of lasting change and performance improvement is popularized by the Arbinger Institute. My figure is based on a figure available on the institute's UK website (https://www.arbingerinstitute.uk/about.html). I simplified the figure to save place here.

[6] The project model, described in the Project Management Body of Knowledge Guide (PMBOK Guide) maintained by the Project Management Institute, meets this requirement. Find out more at https://www.pmi.org/pmbok-guide-standards However, another book, Visualizing Project Management is better to understand the conceptual model of projects.
(Forsberg, Kevin, Hal Mooz, and Howard Cotterman. Visualizing Project Management: Models and Frameworks for Mastering Complex Systems, 3rd ed. (Hoboken, NJ: Josh Wiley & Sons, 2005)

[7] Boleman, Lee G. And Terrence E. Deal. Reframing organizations: Artistry, choice, and leadership, 2nd ed. (San Francisco: Jossey-Bass Publishers, 1997).

[8] The Capability Maturity Model Integration (CMMI) framework was developed by the Software Engineering Institute of Carnegie Mellon University on an initiative of the US Department of Defense. Readers can find a brief description of the framework in Ray Kile, "Appendix E Overview of the SEI-CMMI" in Visualizing Project Management: Models and Frameworks for Mastering Complex Systems, 3rd ed., Kevin Forsberg, Hal Mooz, and Howard Cotterman (Hoboken: John Wiley & Sons, 2005).

[9] A good summary of change management activities and stages of change can be found in Cameron, Esther and Mike Green, Making sense of change management: A complete guide to the models, tools and techniques of organizational change, 5th ed. (London: Kogan Page, 2020).

[10] The change agent is a key figure in a change process. For a detailed description of the role see Cameron, Esther and Mike Green, Making sense of change management: A complete guide to the models, tools and techniques of organizational change, 5th ed. (London: KoganPage, 2020), pp. 204-246.

[11] Cameron, Esther and Mike Green, Making sense of change management: A complete guide to the models, tools and techniques of organizational change, 5th ed. (London: KoganPage, 2020), pp. 124-127.

[12] A sign of coming of age of the agile approach is that Project Management Institute, the organization maintaining the iconic handbook Project Management Body of Knowledge published its first agile guide in 2017. The messy nature of the guide's structure also shows the diversity and immaturity of the field.
Project Management Institute, Agile Practical Guide (Newton Square, PA: Project Management Institute, 2017).

[13] Project Management Institute, Agile Practical Guide (Newton Square, PA: Project Management Institute, 2017).

[14] For beginners in agile, Mark C. Layton, SCRUM for Dummies (Wiley, 2015) is an excellent source. Although SCRUM is only one of many agile methods, it is a good reference point to understand concepts widely used in various agile settings.

[15] To understand the intensity of agile projects, keep in mind that the agile approach builds on the tiger teams of large, high-risk, structured projects. Tiger teams are cross-functional teams called to tackle tough obstacles blocking a project. Tiger teams are to crash these obstacles by intense and focused effort.

Develop mindfulness to thrive in a transforming world

Getting Started with Meditation is a fast track introduction to a simple meditation practice that works. Meditation helps millions to reduce stress, face challenges, and live a happier life. Besides, it does not require special skills or abilities, costs only a few minutes of your time a day, and works for everyone. Follow the right practice, and meditation will improve your health, well-being, and help you tackle difficulties in all fields of life.

Meditation is simple, but it takes time to develop a solid practice and see the first results. Follow the wrong practice, and you will be distracted. This book helps you start with a simple, effective practice that you can start now, and customize to your needs when as you gain experience later.

Tom Rozsas
Getting Started with Mediation
is available on Amazon in all markets
or
you can download the e-book version free from
www.tomrozsas.com

Other books by Tom Rozsas

Available on Amazon in all markets

Getting Started with Meditation

Meditation: Creating space